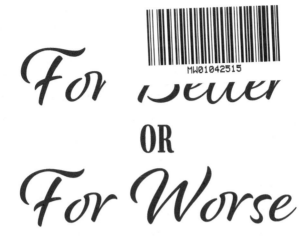

For Better

OR

For Worse

How to Lay an Unshakable
Foundation for a Divorce-proof
Marriage

Prosper Ehunyi

IEM PRESS

PO Box 831001, Richardson, TX 75080
A Subsidiary of IEM APPROACH

IEM PRESS (PO Box 831001, Richardson, TX 75080) functions only as book publisher. As such, the ultimate design, content, editorial accuracy, and views expressed or implied in this work are those of the author. No part of this publication may be reproduced, stored in a retrieval system, or transmitted in any way by any means—electronic, mechanical, photocopy, recording, or otherwise—without the prior permission of the copyright holder, except as provided by USA copyright law. Unless otherwise noted, all Scriptures are taken from the Holy Bible, the New King James Version®. Copyright © 1982 by Thomas Nelson. Used by permission. All rights reserved.zondervan. com ISBN

ISBN 13: 978-1-63603-013-5

Library of Congress
Catalog Card Number: 2020922987

Table of Contents

Dedication

I would like to dedicate this book to Pastor Taku Bessong. Sir, you went against the protocol back in those days in Full Gospel Church Mile 16 in Cameroon to bring me into a class I did not qualify for. Through that class, I was able to catch this revelation, which has never left me, but which has kept hunting me. Today, thank God, I have relieved myself from the burden. Thank you for believing in me and seeing a future I did not see in those days. You gave me lessons and training that have helped me in ministry all these years. Thank you especially for the homiletic class. As a new convert in those days, I did not know why you recommended that class to me, but today I know better.

To my succulent wife, who was in agreement with me during our marriage vows to eliminate for better or for worse.

To Pastor Bridget Israel, who cooperated with us to see this decision accomplished.

Introduction

This book is not to criticize ignorance, but to take ignorance to the place it belongs. Marriage is the most attacked institution by the forces of darkness. This is because they know there is power in oneness. Two is better than one, when those two agree. This book is for the married, singles, youths, and those engaged. It is to help us use our mouths to praise instead of tearing down. *For Better or For Worse* is to help some of God's children to enjoy the full package of God's salvation for us. One of the ways this will be accomplished will be by the power of our tongue. The tongue is a powerful instrument to give life or to kill. And we all want to use it positively and not negatively.

Whosoever uses the tongue wisely will eat the fruits for good or for bad. And those who use it foolishly will also eat the fruits of evil. Therefore, it is very important that we understand what kind of vows we make when we stand before the altar, especially on a wedding day. Marriage is very good if we do it right. If we do it God's way, there will be nothing like divorce or separation. When God says He hates divorce, He means business. The "D" word was never in His original plan. And some of the things most folks confess on their wedding days are actually the causes of most of these divorces. Poverty will lead to the unthinkable. Don't even try to confess it, even with all the faith you have. You will not be able to handle it.

Those who desire to get married should not jump into it if they are not really sick and about to die of loneliness. The reason is because marriage is not just about sex. The young men and women should keep themselves pure and abstain from any kind of sexual impurity. This will pay off in the long run as they enter and stay in the institution of marriage. This book is easy and straight to the point. If there is still something abnormal in your life or marriage after reading this book, please seek deliverance. Some stuff in our lives will only leave with strong prayers and not just through confessions.

In The Beginning It Was Not So

When God created man, He was perfect in all his ways and in every aspect. For the Lord wanted man to be like Him. That means to have God-like attributes.

> In Genesis 1:26-27, *"Then God said, 'Let Us make man in Our image, according to Our likeness; let them have dominion over the fish of the sea, over the birds of the air, and over the cattle, over all the earth and over every creeping thing that creeps on the earth.' So God created man in His own image; in the image of God He created him; male and female He created them."*

It was the plan of God for man to operate with the full potential of His maker. For the Lord even went as far as pronouncing and imparting His authority upon man in order for him to excel on earth. The Lord gave him dominion over all the earth, i.e. you are able to overcome whatever power that may try to challenge you.

In Genesis 1:1, the Bible says, "In the beginning God ..."

So, before the whole process of creation started, God was already on the scene. If He was already on the scene, then grace was there, mercy was there, love was there, compassion was there, goodness was there, and all the attributes of the Lord were there. For when we mention the name of God, His unbeatable attributes immediately come into our minds. So, when we say God, we think of HIS greatness, favor, integrity, dominion, power, and other attributes that portray the nature of God. The Bible did not say in the beginning sickness, poverty, AIDS, malaria, cancer, death, hatred, fear, insecurity, witchcraft, torments, or disasters because these are not found in God and neither are they found in His agenda for man. Do not forget that when God created man, He looked upon man and He said it was good. Genesis 1:31, **"*Then God saw everything that He had made, and indeed* it was *very good. So the evening and the morning were the sixth day."***

When God created man, He was perfect, whole and complete, until iniquity was found in him. Just like the Bible says about Lucifer, in Ezekiel 28:12-19,

> *"Son of man, take up a lamentation for the king of Tyre, and say to him, 'Thus says the Lord GOD: "You were the seal of perfection, / Full of wisdom and perfect in beauty. / You were in Eden, the garden of God; / Every precious stone was your covering: / The sardius, topaz, and diamond, / Beryl, onyx, and jasper, / Sapphire, turquoise, and emerald with gold. / The workmanship of your timbrels and pipes / Was prepared for you on the day you were created.*

> *"You were the anointed cherub who covers; / I established you; / You were on the holy mountain of God; / You walked back and forth in the midst of fiery stones. / You were perfect in your ways from the day you were created, / Till iniquity was found in you.*

> *"By the abundance of your trading / You became filled with violence within, / And you sinned; / Therefore I cast you as a profane thing / Out of the mountain of God; / And I destroyed you, O covering cherub, / From the midst of the fiery stones.*

"Your heart was lifted up because of your beauty; / You corrupted your wisdom for the sake of your splendor; / I cast you to the ground, / I laid you before kings, / That they might gaze at you."

"You defiled your sanctuaries / By the multitude of your iniquities, / By the iniquity of your trading; / Therefore I brought fire from your midst; / It devoured you, / And I turned you to ashes upon the earth / In the sight of all who saw you. / All who knew you among the peoples are astonished at you; / You have become a horror, / And shall be *no more forever."""*

For those of you who are asking why God created Satan, I want you to know that God did not create Satan. He created Lucifer, which means "light bearer." He was perfect in beauty and in all his ways. He was son of light. He was son of the morning.

Isaiah 14:12-16: "How you are fallen from heaven, / O Lucifer, son of the morning! / How *you are cut down to the ground, / You who weakened the nations! / For you have said in your heart: / 'I will ascend into heaven, / I will exalt my throne above the stars of God; / I will also sit on the mount of the congregation / On the farthest sides of the north. / I will ascend above the heights*

of the clouds, / I will be like the Most High.'
/ Yet you shall be brought down to Sheol, /
To the lowest depths of the Pit.

"Those who see you will gaze at you, / And
consider you, saying: / 'Is *this the man*
who made the earth tremble, / Who shook
kingdoms?'"

He had greatness, power, dominion, beauty;
I mean, he had it all. Therefore, he was able to
launch a coup d'état against God. He succeeded
and swayed about one-third of God's angels
against the Lord. He lured them to join him in
his wicked plan. He was cast down with these
angels. Thereafter, he became known as Satan, or
devil, meaning adversary, opponent, accuser, and
prosecutor.

Revelation 12:7-10: "And war broke out in
heaven: Michael and his angels fought with
the dragon; and the dragon and his angels
fought, but they did not prevail, nor was a
place found for them in heaven any longer.
So the great dragon was cast out, that
serpent of old, called the Devil and Satan,
who deceives the whole world; he was cast
to the earth, and his angels were cast out
with him.

"Then I heard a loud voice saying in heaven, 'Now salvation, and strength, and the kingdom of our God, and the power of His Christ have come, for the accuser of our brethren, who accused them before our God day and night, has been cast down.' "

He became an enemy to the Almighty God and to whatever pertained to Him (E.g. man). He knew sins separated man from God.

Isaiah 59:1, *"Behold, the LORD's hand is not shortened, / That it cannot save; / Nor His ear heavy, / That it cannot hear. / But your iniquities have separated you from your God; / And your sins have hidden* **His** *face from you, / So that He will not hear."*

From that time, he became the accuser of the brethren and mankind. He was the god of this world (and he still is; see 2 Corinthians 4:4). He is here to interrupt and disrupt God's work as much as he can.

Mark 4:15: *"And these are the ones by the wayside where the word is sown. When they hear, Satan comes immediately and takes away the word that was sown in their hearts."*

Why? To make men to turn away from the Lord of Lords (Job 2:4-5).

To take away God's worship from men (Luke 4:6-8).

Therefore, he began eyeing man from the day God kept him in the garden and gave him dominion. The devil, or Satan, was not happy, because he knew what he had lost. He began devising plans to take human beings away from their God—a task he is faithfully committed to even today. He finally succeeded when man sinned against God.

When man sinned against the Most High, mankind was separated from God. Man fell from the realm of dominion and perfection. Sin now opens the doors to the devil to come in with his stuff. The opportunity he had been waiting for was given to him. He was ready to let God know he was not going to suffer in hell alone. That was how the devil came in with his sicknesses and diseases, poverty, accidents, death, hatred and witchcraft, and all the sufferings and yokes that men go through. Mankind was separated from God and became vulnerable to his attacks. Man fell from grace to grass.

1 John 5:19, *"We know that we are of God, and the whole world lies under the sway of the wicked one."*

Genesis 3:16-19, *"To the woman He said: / 'I will greatly multiply your sorrow and your conception; / In pain you shall bring forth children; / Your desire* shall be *for your husband, / And he shall rule over you.'*

"Then to Adam He said, 'Because you have heeded the voice of your wife, and have eaten from the tree of which I commanded you, saying, 'You shall not eat of it': / Cursed is *the ground for your sake; / In toil you shall eat* of *it / All the days of your life. / Both thorns and thistles it shall bring forth for you, / And you shall eat the herb of the field. / In the sweat of your face you shall eat bread / Till you return to the ground, / For out of it you were taken; / For dust you* are, */ And to dust you shall return."*

(Wow! This sounds like in sickness and in lack. And the people will answer yes. God will punish Satan.)

Remember that prior to the fall, man was perfect and was having good times with the Lord. There was no sorrow or sadness. There was no mourning or crying, and neither was there poverty nor depression.

Genesis.2:15-16, *"Then the LORD God took the man and put him in the garden of Eden to tend and keep it. And the LORD God commanded the man, saying, 'Of every tree of the garden you may freely eat.'"*

Today there is nothing like freedom without Christ. Freedom is only found when we give our lives to Christ. Our Father's original intentions were for everyone to have a work to do while all would be consummated in worship—like in the days of the American revival, whereby men would take their lunch breaks and go to the house of God to worship. So the plan was (without sin coming into place) for us to freely enjoy what we did while worshipping and not going to so-called work with a long face or discontentment. That is bondage.

The Father's thought toward us are for good and not for evil (Jeremiah 29:11). If He thinks good about me, why must I turn around and think evil in my own future? Why must I become a prophet of evil over my life?

Genesis 1:26-31: *"Then God said, 'Let Us make man in Our image, according to Our likeness; let them have dominion over the fish of the sea, over the birds of the air, and over the cattle, over all the earth and over every creeping thing that creeps on the* *earth.' So God created man in His* own *image; in the image of God He created him; male and female He created them. Then God blessed them, and God said to them, 'Be fruitful and multiply; fill the earth and subdue it; have dominion over the fish of the sea, over the birds of the air, and over every living thing that moves on the earth.'*

"And God said, 'See, I have given you every herb that *yields seed which* is *on the face of all the earth, and every tree whose fruit yields seed; to you it shall be for food. Also, to every beast of the earth, to every bird of the air, and to everything that creeps on the earth, in which* there is *life,* I have given *every green herb for food'; and it was so. Then God saw everything that He had made, and indeed* it was *very good. So the evening and the morning were the sixth day."*

Man did not wake up one morning with back pain, headaches, sickness, or flu. Because of sin, today we have AIDS, coronavirus, and many more diseases that were not there in the beginning. Man was having a great time with his Lord. For all that the Lord made was good and pleasant—even the animals. So it was not the plan of God that men should carry sicknesses. Sickness is not even in His vocabulary or dictionary. For the plan He has for us is a plan of good, and not of evil, and is to give us a future and a hope. That will mean a plan to prosper us and to enlarge our coast.

There is No Poverty with God

Poverty is from the pit of hell, and it is a result of a lack of knowledge. Our Father is not poor. He is all sufficient God (El-Shaddai). There is no such thing as "poverty is next to godliness." We can't afford to be poor when there is so much for us to do with money when spreading the good news of the kingdom. That is why the devil is fighting every true believer financially. He also knows that if we are financially broke, we will easily give in to temptations. For the love of money is the root of all evils (1 Timothy 6:10). A true believer who is financially loaded will not easily be enticed to compromise their convictions in relation to one who is struggling financially. The bottom line is that every true believer must fight poverty. And the first step is: do not confess that you will be poor. If we will obey and serve God, He will supply our needs according to His riches in glory. We shall surely eat the good of the land (Isaiah 1:19).

Job 36:11: *"If they obey and serve Him, / They shall spend their days in prosperity, / And their years in pleasures."*

For the good Lord takes pleasure in the prosperity of His sons and daughters (Psalm 35:27). If He takes pleasure in it, then it is not His will for us to be broke. Poverty is not next to godliness; instead, it gives the devil a big mouth to mock our God with. We are also vulnerable to all kinds of satanic enticements.

2

The Confessions

Your Confession Will Make You or Kill You – Part 1

Therefore, when a man and a woman or couples who are about to get married stand before the Lord or before the altar and make a vow, they actually design their destiny from that point. The solidity of the marriage will be based on the confession they made before the Lord on that faithful day. For confession is made unto salvation—it can either kill you or make you. It can kill the marriage or make the marriage.

The confession "for better or for worse" is not found in the Bible. There is nowhere in the Bible that the Lord said during a wedding ceremony that we should pledge for better or for worse. Just look at the synonyms for worse: most awful, most horrible, wickedest—these are all synonyms. Is there anywhere in the Bible that God said to us or to a prophet that during a marriage ceremony His children should confess for better or for worse? I know, just as you know, that the answer is no. Let's take a look at marriage ceremonies and issues on marriage in the Old Testament and New Testament.

Some Marriage Scenarios

Genesis 2:24, *"Therefore a man shall leave his father and mother and be joined to his wife, and they shall become one flesh."*

This is one Scripture that I personally think that if the Lord Almighty wanted for us to use for "better or for worse," He should have added it to this. And the Scripture should have read thus, "And they shall become one flesh for better or for worse and in sickness and in poverty."

Genesis 24:60 (KJV), *"And they blessed Rebekah, and said unto her, Thou art our sister, be thou the mother of thousands of millions, and let thy seed possess the gate of those which hate them."*

Rebekah's parents did not mention that which relates to the curse brought to us by Adam and Eve. They wanted their daughter to succeed and enjoy her marriage. Rebekah's parents blessed her for the best. No right-thinking parents would pronounce sufferings on their children (even though we know it exists) before sending them on a mission. Neither my parents nor my wife's parents did such a thing during our traditional wedding ceremony. They wished us the best in our marriage. Not in sicknesses or in poverty. Of course, if we are in sicknesses or poverty, then our parents will also get a piece of this. And if we are in health or in riches, they will also enjoy this with us.

The curses listed in Deuteronomy 28 were meant for the children of disobedience, or those who operated in disobedience. And I know you are not one of them. **But if you are, please quickly repent today.**

Deuteronomy 28:15-52: "But it shall come to pass, if you do not obey the voice of the LORD your God, to observe carefully all His commandments and His statutes which I command you today, that all these curses will come upon you and overtake you:

"Cursed shall you be in the city, and cursed shall you be in the country.

"Cursed shall be *your basket and your kneading bowl.*

"Cursed shall be *the fruit of your body and the produce of your land, the increase of your cattle and the offspring of your flocks.*

"Cursed shall *you* be *when you come in, and cursed* shall *you* be *when you go out.*

"The LORD will send on you cursing, confusion, and rebuke in all that you set your hand to do, until you are destroyed and until you perish quickly, because of the wickedness of your doings in which you have forsaken Me. The LORD will make the plague cling to you until He has consumed you from the land which you are going to possess. The LORD will strike you with consumption, with fever, with inflammation, with severe burning fever, with the sword, with scorching, and with mildew; they shall pursue you until you perish. And your heavens which are *over your head shall be bronze, and the earth which is under you* shall be *iron. The LORD will change the rain of your land to powder and dust; from the heaven it shall come down on you until you are destroyed.*

"The LORD will cause you to be defeated before your enemies; you shall go out one way against them and flee seven ways before them; and you shall become troublesome to all the kingdoms of the earth. Your carcasses shall be food for all the birds of the air and the beasts of the earth, and no one shall frighten them *away. The LORD will strike you with the boils of Egypt, with tumors, with the scab, and with the itch, from which you cannot be healed. The LORD will strike you with madness and blindness and confusion of heart. And you shall grope at noonday, as a blind man gropes in darkness; you shall not prosper in your ways; you shall be only oppressed and plundered continually, and no one shall save* you.

"You shall betroth a wife, but another man shall lie with her; you shall build a house, but you shall not dwell in it; you shall plant a vineyard, but shall not gather its grapes. Your ox shall be *slaughtered before your eyes, but you shall not eat of it; your donkey* shall be *violently taken away from before you, and shall not be restored to you; your sheep* shall be *given to your enemies, and you shall have no one to rescue* them. *Your sons and your daughters* shall be *given to another people, and your eyes shall look*

and fail with longing *for them all day long; and* there shall be *no strength in your hand. A nation whom you have not known shall eat the fruit of your land and the produce of your labor, and you shall be only oppressed and crushed continually. So you shall be driven mad because of the sight which your eyes see. The LORD will strike you in the knees and on the legs with severe boils which cannot be healed, and from the sole of your foot to the top of your head.*

"The LORD will bring you and the king whom you set over you to a nation which neither you nor your fathers have known, and there you shall serve other gods— wood and stone. And you shall become an astonishment, a proverb, and a byword among all nations where the LORD will drive you.

"You shall carry much seed out to the field but gather little in, for the locusts shall consume it. You shall plant vineyards and tend them, *but you shall neither drink of the wine nor gather the* grapes; *for the worms shall eat them. You shall have olive trees throughout all your territory, but you shall not anoint* yourself *with the oil; for your olives shall drop off. You shall beget*

sons and daughters, but they shall not be yours; for they shall go into captivity. Locusts shall consume all your trees and the produce of your land.

"The alien who is among you shall rise higher and higher above you, and you shall come down lower and lower. He shall lend to you, but you shall not lend to him; he shall be the head, and you shall be the tail.

"Moreover all these curses shall come upon you and pursue and overtake you, until you are destroyed, because you did not obey the voice of the LORD your God, to keep His commandments and His statutes which He commanded you. And they shall be upon you for a sign and a wonder, and on your descendants forever.

"Because you did not serve the LORD your God with joy and gladness of heart, for the abundance of everything, therefore you shall serve your enemies, whom the LORD will send against you, in hunger, in thirst, in nakedness, and in need of everything; and He will put a yoke of iron on your neck until He has destroyed you. The LORD will bring a nation against you from afar, from the end of the earth, as swift *as the eagle*

flies, a nation whose language you will not understand, a nation of fierce countenance, which does not respect the elderly nor show favor to the young. And they shall eat the increase of your livestock and the produce of your land, until you are destroyed; they shall not leave you grain or new wine or oil, or *the increase of your cattle or the offspring of your flocks, until they have destroyed you."*

"They shall besiege you at all your gates until your high and fortified walls, in which you trust, come down throughout all your land; and they shall besiege you at all your gates throughout all your land which the LORD your God has given you."

And the list goes on. If you are going to live your life in disobedience and in rebellion, then you can claim or take a vow with curses attached to it. But as for me and my house, we have suffered enough. I am not ready to add more to it with my own confession. After all, the devil will still try to attack, so why make it so legal and easy for him?

But if you are an obedient child of God, then blessings are meant for you. That is what the minister needs to declare over obedient children of God.

Deuteronomy 28:1-14, "Now it shall come to pass, if you diligently obey the voice of the **LORD** your God, to observe carefully all His commandments which I command you today, that the **LORD** your God will set you high above all nations of the earth. *And all these blessings shall come upon you and overtake you, because you obey the voice of the LORD your God:*

"Blessed shall *you* be *in the city, and blessed* shall *you* be *in the country.*

"Blessed shall be *the fruit of your body, the produce of your ground and the increase of your herds, the increase of your cattle and the offspring of your flocks.*

"Blessed shall be *your basket and your kneading bowl.*

"Blessed shall *you* be *when you come in, and blessed* shall *you* be *when you go out.*

"The LORD will cause your enemies who rise against you to be defeated before your face; they shall come out against you one way and flee before you seven ways.

"The LORD will command the blessing on you in your storehouses and in all to which you set your hand, and He will bless you in the land which the LORD your God is giving you.

"The LORD will establish you as a holy people to Himself, just as He has sworn to you, if you keep the commandments of the LORD your God and walk in His ways. Then all peoples of the earth shall see that you are called by the name of the LORD, and they shall be afraid of you. And the LORD will grant you plenty of goods, in the fruit of your body, in the increase of your livestock, and in the produce of your ground, in the land of which the LORD swore to your fathers to give you. The LORD will open to you His good treasure, the heavens, to give the rain to your land in its season, and to bless all the work of your hand. You shall lend to many nations, but you shall not borrow. And the LORD will make you the head and not the tail; you shall be above only, and not be beneath, if you heed the commandments of the LORD your God, which I command you today, and are careful to observe them. *So you shall not turn aside from any of the words which I command you this day,* to

the right or the left, to go after other gods to serve them."

In Ephesians 5:24-32, we are shown that marriage is figurative of Christ marrying the church, for there will be no marriage in heaven. I do not see or hear Christ making any negative vow before marrying the church.

The thought that God has concerning us from the beginning is a thought for good and not for evil. For better or for worse was not in existence in the beginning.

Matthew 19:8, ***"He said to them, 'Moses, because of the hardness of your hearts, permitted you to divorce your wives, but from the beginning it was not so.'"***

Just like divorce, it was after the fall of man that in sickness and in poverty, or in death and in lack, came in—in the beginning it was not so. God never intended or asked man to go through this bondage-binding confession. The church is following after the court system of this world instead of taking advantage of the finished work of Calvary. The church is supposed to be the light for the world to follow, not vice versa. When I came across this revelation, I then realized why there is an alarming rate of divorce in the body of Christ. The accuser of the brethren fights Christian marriages more than those of unbelievers. He knows a dysfunctional home will lead to a dysfunctional society. When the bride says, "I do" and the groom says, "I will" or "I do," then they open themselves up to the side of the confession that belongs to the devil. (This part is a result of the fall of man and is the devil's responsibility to fulfill.) That negative part of the confession is a legal and undisputable invitation for Satan. The devil can now pick up the negative part of the confession and begin to oppress their lives even during their honeymoon. The moon that is supposed to be full with honey will create sorrow, bitterness, and regrets. Why? Because the devil is Mr. Worst.

He is the guy behind all the evil, the lack, the poverty, the deaths, and the sicknesses. Nothing good comes from him. Even before the couples leave the honey in the moon (honeymoon), they already have serious resentments and disappointments about their marriage because the accuser of the brethren has started playing his role in their confession or covenant. The devil goes before God and says something like, "Sister A and Brother B said for worse and for worst— you know what, I have started afflicting them already financially, sexually, and emotionally, and I am still planning to do the worst."

This is how so many of the newly wedded have used their own mouths to invite the ministry of warfare into their marital homes. As soon as they leave the honeymoon, it will be warfare throughout. I have heard a brother calling the pastor right from the honeymoon location to cry bitterly about how things have turned the other way around. The honey has become bitter. The devil has dealt with their productivity or fruitfulness. There are many of you who know of folks who have divorced immediately after their honeymoons. Some receive the seed of divorce even before the honeymoon and carry it along the highway of marriage until it germinates, grows, and matures.

Remember, divorce is not in the original plan of the MOST HIGH. It is as a result of sin. See Matthew 19:8. The Lord says in Malachi 2:16 that He hates divorce. And when God says He hates something, it means it is a sin. For as long as this man called the devil is still around, we are in a continuous war. First Peter 5:8, John 10:10, Revelation 12:10, and Job 1:6: write out some of these Scriptures for yourself.

The devil is the prosecutor against Christians. He takes all evidence (be it verbal or nonverbal) before God about why we must not be blessed. Many Christians, after making such confessions, unfortunately or ignorantly take off the whole armor of God instead of putting it on. Many have taken the back seat to relax while the devil is making a mess out of their marital homes. He was not foolish when he attacked the first marriage in the garden of Eden. He knew good marriages mean a better society.

I am not saying good marriages have no trials. Acts 14:22 says that trials and persecutions will come, but let it be for the sake of the gospel or righteousness not due to our own lack of knowledge or negligence.

Hosea 4:6 and 1 Peter 3:17 and 4:15 say attacks from hell due to this confession will not be considered sufferings for Christ but due to ignorance.

In the Bible, Job was partly the cause of his own dilemma. He had fear in his life. He was so afraid about his children. And where there is fear, there is no faith. And fear has given the devil legal rights to afflict so many Christians. For fear is not of God, but faith is. For by faith, God is being glorified. When the devil finds fear in a Christian, that believer is vulnerable to his assaults. When Peter began to be afraid, he began sinking (Matthew 14:30). The suffering of Job was also connected to his fears. The devil saw the loophole.

Job 1:5, *"So it was, when the days of feasting had run their course, that Job would send and sanctify them, and he would rise early in the morning and offer burnt offerings* according to *the number of them all. For Job said, 'It may be that my sons have sinned and cursed God in their hearts.' Thus Job did regularly."*

Job 3:25, *"For the thing I greatly feared has come upon me, / And what I dreaded has happened to me."*

Job was ensnared by the confessions of his own mouth. Out of fear, what he regularly confessed befell him. Some Christians still live their lives as if they are still under the law. Their holiness is not born out of love. Faith worketh by love. Fear worketh by law.

Some years ago, a brother died in Deeper Life Church because he was so afraid of the threats of a man that told him because you have married my wife, (i.e. a woman he was thinking of marrying but who had left the world and given her life to Christ) you will see! The brother went and told his pastor that, "These people are wicked oh." And when this evil man shot the arrow, it got him. For he kept confessing, "These people are wicked, oh."

Therefore, the Bible says, above all, put on the shield of faith that is able to quench all the fiery darts of the evil one (Ephesians 6:16).

For the devil saw a man who was devoted to God but who had fear. Suffering was not in the original plan of God for man, so why will you use your mouth to invite it into your marriage? If it comes of its own accord, that is different. Why call for it? That is double trouble.

God Against Negative Confessions: The Twelve Spies

> Numbers 13:26-33, *"Now they departed and came back to Moses and Aaron and all the congregation of the children of Israel in the Wilderness of Paran, at Kadesh; they brought back word to them and to all the congregation, and showed them the fruit of the land. Then they told him, and said: 'We went to the land where you sent us. It truly flows with milk and honey, and this* is *its fruit. Nevertheless the people who dwell in the land* are *strong; the cities* are *fortified* and *very large; moreover we saw the descendants of Anak there. The Amalekites dwell in the land of the South; the Hittites, the Jebusites, and the Amorites dwell in the*

mountains; and the Canaanites dwell by the sea and along the banks of the Jordan.'

"Then Caleb quieted the people before Moses, and said, 'Let us go up at once and take possession, for we are well able to overcome it.'

"But the men who had gone up with him said, 'We are not able to go up against the people, for they are *stronger than we.' And they gave the children of Israel a bad report of the land which they had spied out, saying, 'The land through which we have gone as spies* is *a land that devours its inhabitants, and all the people whom we saw in it* are *men of* great *stature. There we saw the giants (the descendants of Anak came from the giants); and we were like grasshoppers in our own sight, and so we were in their sight.'"*

The Bible says that we are ensnared by the words of our mouth (Proverbs 6:2).

The story of the spies tells us that ten out of the twelve spies brought negative reports, and they even went as far as calling themselves grasshoppers. And indeed, they died like grasshoppers in the wilderness while God satisfied Caleb and Joshua with long life. At eighty years, Caleb was still strong and enjoying the land flowing with milk and honey because of his confession while the others who called themselves grasshoppers received the life span of grasshoppers.

> **Numbers 14:26-30,** *"And the LORD spoke to Moses and Aaron, saying, 'How long* shall I bear with *this evil congregation who complain against Me? I have heard the complaints which the children of Israel make against Me. Say to them, "As I live,"* says the LORD, *"just as you have spoken in My hearing, so I will do to you: The carcasses of you who have complained against Me shall fall in this wilderness, all of you who were numbered, according to your entire number, from twenty years old and above. Except for Caleb the son of Jephunneh and Joshua the son of Nun, you shall by no means enter the land which I swore I would make you dwell in."'"*

God had already proposed from the beginning—in fact, He was determined from the outset—to give them blessing. But they used their own mouths to talk themselves out of it. We sadden His heart when we give the devil legal rights to hold us ransom before Him and show the Lord why He should not bless us. The Lord had no choice but to do to them as they had said. As for me and my household, I will be of a different spirit. I will not accept unbiblical pronunciations, confessions, and vows because so many are accepting it. I will be like my brothers (Caleb and Joshua) whereby I know there are troubles out there, but I will not confess it. Yes, there are diseases, sicknesses, and whatever, but I will not confess them. I will not allow the Lord to be sad with me for speaking contrarily to His Word.

> **Numbers 14:24,** *"But My servant Caleb, because he has a different spirit in him and has followed Me fully, I will bring into the land where he went, and his descendants shall inherit it."*

Covenanted Bonding: Spiritual Significance, Power of Words, Implications – Part 2

Consider Romans 10:10. So what kind of confession do you want to do? Unto salvation i.e. freedom, deliverance, liberty, or unto bondage? Listen, life and death are in the power of the tongue.

> **Proverb 18:21,** *"Death and life* are *in the power of the tongue, / And those who love it will eat its fruit."*

Our tongue will either lead us to heaven or hell. It can either kill us or save us. The choice is ours.

The Bible says in **Matthew 16:19,** *"And I will give you the keys of the kingdom of heaven, and whatever you bind on earth will be bound in heaven, and whatever you loose on earth will be loosed in heaven."*

This verse actually means that whatever we allow on earth, God will allow, and whatever we disallow on earth, He will also disallow. This is the kind of dominion He gave us when He created us. We can either use the power to bind ourselves or to loose ourselves. The Lord has given you the power already. For don't you know, He has made us a little lower than angels? And He says, Don't you know you are gods? (See John 10:34-35, Psalm 8:5-6.)

Therefore, do not allow any preacher or pastor to put you into any bondage that will shape your marital destiny in a hard way. For you are your own prophets. You are the first prophet of your life. You have the power to prophesy doom to your future or life. Of course life is what you want it to be because that is what the Lord Jesus came that we should have and have it more abundantly (John 10:10b).

The Word says in **3 John 1:2,** *"Beloved, I pray that you may prosper in all things and be in health, just as your soul prospers."*

So where is for better or for worse coming from? Well, as a man thinketh, so is he, and as he maketh his bed, so shall he lie on it.

The declarations and the things you will do in life have far-reaching effects and consequences. For you will declare a thing and it shall be established for you (Job 22:28). The declaration that Isaac made toward Jacob and Esau could not be reversed, even though Esau cried and tried hard to get a blessing. The words Jacob spoke on his son before he died were effective on them (Genesis 49). The Lord said that the words that He spoke to us, they are life and spirit (John 6:63). Our word is spirit, and when it goes out, you can't retrieve it. It goes into the atmosphere and creates its results, which are either negative or positive. It can bring life or death. There is power in the spoken word. Do not underestimate your words.

2 Kings 6:18, *"So when the Syrians came down to him, Elisha prayed to the LORD, and said, 'Strike this people, I pray, with blindness.' And He struck them with blindness according to the word of Elisha."*

Word creates. **Psalm 33:6: *"By the word of the LORD the heavens were made, / And all the host of them by the breath of His mouth."***

Words bring healing and deliverance, according to Psalm 107:20.

During marriages, the vows we make have far-reaching implications. A **vow** is a voluntary pledge to fulfill an agreement. There are a lot of instances in the Bible whereby individuals took vows and then they were bound by those vows. A vow, in other words, is a binding agreement. People bind themselves with vows, which they either have to fulfill or break or the divine, supernatural power of God releases them from it. It might be ok right now because of grace. But should we continue to live in ignorance?

Numbers 30:1-7, *"Then Moses spoke to the heads of the tribes concerning the children of Israel, saying, 'This is the thing which the LORD has commanded: If a man makes a vow to the LORD, or swears an oath to bind himself by some agreement, he shall not break his word; he shall do according to all that proceeds out of his mouth.*

"'Or if a woman makes a vow to the LORD, and binds herself *by some agreement while in her father's house in her youth, and her father hears her vow and the agreement by which she has bound herself, and her father holds his peace, then all her vows shall stand, and every agreement with which she has bound herself shall stand. But if her father overrules her on the day that he hears, then none of her vows nor her agreements by which she has bound herself shall stand; and the LORD will release her, because her father overruled her.*

"'If indeed she takes a husband, while bound by her vows or by a rash utterance from her lips by which she bound herself, and her husband hears it, *and makes no response to her on the day that he hears, then her vows shall stand, and her agreements by which she bound herself shall stand.'"*

Genesis 28:20-22: *"Then Jacob made a vow, saying, 'If God will be with me, and keep me in this way that I am going, and give me bread to eat and clothing to put on, so that I come back to my father's house in peace, then the LORD shall be my God. And this stone which I have set as a pillar shall be*

God's house, and of all that You give me I will surely give a tenth to You.'"

1 Samuel 1:11, *"Then she made a vow and said, 'O LORD of hosts, if You will indeed look on the affliction of Your maidservant and remember me, and not forget Your maidservant, but will give Your maidservant a male child, then I will give him to the LORD all the days of his life, and no razor shall come upon his head.'"*

The Bible teaches that when we make a vow, we should fulfill it (Ecclesiastes 5:4-6). Remember, when you speak a vow, it jumps into the realm of the spirit. It's being heard (Psalm 61:5). The marital vow for better or for worse, in poverty and in sicknesses, in sufferings and in death and so on is a binding agreement between couples. But the devil had to fulfill his part in this vow, which of course is the negative part. And because you have spoken it and agreed on it, he does not waste any time to begin operations. He immediately comes in with a spirit of poverty, barrenness, infidelity, death, sicknesses, and all the other sufferings and evils you can think of.

And he who sits on the throne cries out, "These people are suffering for lack of knowledge." *For ignorance is not an excuse for bondage.* The youths who mocked Elisha thought they were having fun, but little did they know they would become "friedhof gemuse" (graveyard vegetables/corpses).

These marital vows have ensnared many folks and will still ensnare ignorant folks. What about you? Do you want to join the number? **Proverbs 6:2,** *"You are snared by the words of your mouth; / You are taken by the words of your mouth."* The groom and the bride should instead release the honey and the milk under their tongues (Song of Solomon 4:11) into their marriages: *"Your lips, O* my *spouse, / Drip as the honeycomb; / Honey and milk* are *under your tongue; / And the fragrance of your garments /* Is *like the fragrance of Lebanon."* Don't get me wrong: I know believers will go through tribulations (Acts 14:22), but that is different from believers who give the devil the legal rights to afflict their lives because of ignorance and lack of knowledge. This is what deliverance ministers call self-imposed curses.

3

The Price Paid For Our Restoration

I am a firm believer that the package for my salvation was complete. It was total!

The curse in the garden: the curse of suffering

> Genesis 3:16-19, "*To the woman, He said: / 'I will greatly multiply your sorrow and your conception; / In pain you shall bring forth children; / Your desire shall be for your husband, / and he shall rule over you.'*
>
> "*Then to Adam He said, 'Because you have heeded the voice of your wife, and have eaten from the tree of which I commanded you, saying, 'You shall not eat of it': /*

Cursed is *the ground for your sake; / In toil you shall eat of it / All the days of your life. / Both thorns and thistles it shall bring forth for you, / And you shall eat the herb of the field. / In the sweat of your face you shall eat bread / Till you return to the ground, / For out of it you were taken; / For dust you are, / And to dust you shall return.*"

In Genesis 3, man was introduced to suffering. Sin separated man from God. The Lord was disappointed. But because of His love for man, He had to call for the lamb that was slain before the foundation of the world.

Revelation 13:8, *"All who dwell on the earth will worship him, whose names have not been written in the Book of Life of the Lamb slain from the foundation of the world."*

The Lord told Jesus to get ready because it was time to go down on earth to rescue His people as it had been agreed upon. The Lord had provision ready, for He knew what was going to happen to man.

The Finished Work of the Son

Colossians 1:13-14, *"He has delivered us from the power of darkness and conveyed* us *into the kingdom of the Son of His love, in whom we have redemption through His blood, the forgiveness of sins."*

So, God gave away His only begotten son (John 3:16) to restore man back to God. The restoration process was completed when Christ, hanging on the cross, cried out, "It is finished," and died. As soon as He did that, the curse of suffering was broken, and man was restored back to his heavenly Father and to his original place of the God-kind of life. A life of peace, joy, righteousness, abundance, prosperity, good health, and every nature or attribute given to man that pertains to the Almighty.

For it is written, cursed is he who hangeth on the tree.

Galatians 3:13-14, *"Christ has redeemed us from the curse of the law, having become a curse for us (for it is written, 'Cursed is everyone who hangs on a tree'), that the blessing of Abraham might come upon the*

Gentiles in Christ Jesus, that we might receive the promise of the Spirit through faith."

So God gave away His only son for the Adamic curse. For Christ had rescued us from the curse of the law "that the blessing of Abraham might come upon the Gentiles in Christ Jesus, that we might receive the promise of the Spirit through faith." Therefore, on the cross of Calvary, He took away the curses of sickness, disease, death, poverty, and condemnation. So that the blessings of Abraham might come upon us (you also), which are multiplication, fruitfulness, riches, a long life, good health, and all the goodness of God. For the Bible records that Jesus became poor that we might be rich.

2 Corinthians 8:9, *"For you know the grace of our Lord Jesus Christ, that though He was rich, yet for your sakes He became poor, that you through His poverty might become rich."*

On the cross, Christ was reconciling men back to God. He was justifying men before God and bestowing upon them His gift of righteousness.

2 Corinthians 5:16-18, *"Therefore, from now on, we regard no one according to the* *flesh. Even though we have known Christ according to the flesh, yet now we know* Him thus *no longer. Therefore, if anyone* is *in Christ,* he is *a new creation; old things have passed away; behold, all things have become new. Now all things* are *of God, who has reconciled us to Himself through Jesus Christ, and has given us the ministry of reconciliation."*

Romans 5:10-19 tells us He gave back our right to be called children of the Most High God.

John 1:12, *"But as many as received Him, to them He gave the right to become children of God, to those who believe in His name."*

For He was a life-giving spirit (1 Corinthians 15:45). Man died spiritually through the sin of Adam, but we were made alive by Jesus.

1 Corinthians 15:22, *"For as in Adam all die, even so in Christ all shall be made alive."*

For through one's mistakes and errors we were cut off from God, through one man's righteous act, we were restored.

> **Romans 5:18,** *"Therefore, as through one man's offense judgment came to all men, resulting in condemnation, even so through one Man's righteous act the free gift came to all men, resulting in justification of life."*

For if any man is in Christ, old things have passed away and all has become new (2 Corinthians 5:17). Therefore, why would you want to afflict yourself with sufferings which Jesus has already paid the price for? All you need is faith in the atonement, in the blood, and in the finished work on the cross. That which Adam lost through sin and the curse or suffering was restored by the Lord Jesus (Romans 5:10-19). The Lord Jesus took away all the curses, sufferings, and pains that were written against us and wiped them away with His blood.

He took that which was a terror to our life and nailed these things to the cross. He disarmed the devil, beat him up, and gave us our victory (see Colossians 2:14-15, 1 Corinthians 15:57).

> **Colossians 2:13-15,** *"And you, being dead in your trespasses and the uncircumcision of your flesh, He has made alive together with Him, having forgiven you all trespasses, having wiped out the handwriting of requirements that was against us, which was contrary to us. And He has taken it*

out of the way, having nailed it to the cross. Having disarmed principalities and powers, He made a public spectacle of them, triumphing over them in it."

Therefore, there is no reason why a child of God should accept self-affliction. For this is the reason why *"the Son of God was manifested, that He might destroy the works of the devil"* **(1 John 3:8)**. See also Hebrews 2:14.

Now, if you have already taken those negative vows on your wedding day, it is not too late for you to renounce them. Cry out to the Lord just as the Israelites did, and the Lord will hear you. Ask the Lord to forgive your ignorance. Use the blood of Jesus to cancel the vows, the declarations, and the pronouncements.

Reverse the vow and say it in your own way. Prophesy and declare the goodness of God. Remember that there is milk and honey under your tongue (Song of Solomon 4:11). Also greater is He that is in you, and you are power packed (1 John 4:4, Ephesians 3:20-21, Matthew 18:19)

Confess the riches of God (2 Corinthians 9:8) and fruitfulness (Genesis 1:27-29, Psalms 126:3, 128:2-4). Revoke the curses and declare His will upon your marriage. Declare that which is written concerning you in the volumes of the book in heaven. For he that finds a wife obtains **favor** from the Lord, not troubles (Proverbs 18:22).

Favor is the grace (power) of God that brings His visitation in our lives to cause miracles (Genesis 18:3). It also means kindness. Favor will cause men to beg you. It brings prosperity (Genesis 39:21). As children of God, there is an anointing in us to prosper, to grow big, and to enlarge our coast. Favor takes us higher and makes us in charge. It brings an exact, perfect fulfillment of God's promises into our lives. Favor will reverse all the plans of your enemies back to them (Esther 8:5-16). The favor of God is a shield around us. It brings God's divine protection (Psalms 5:12, 30:5). There is so much to the word favor and what it will do. So marriage is a blessing to be enjoyed.

For the blessings of the Lord make you rich and adds no sorrow (Proverbs 10:22). Marriage is a blessing. A wife is supposed to be sweet, like honey (Proverbs 24:13). I will not use my tongue to make it bitter. Confess Psalm 71:21: For the Lord will increase your greatness and comfort you on every side. Declare Psalms 105:37 and 90:14-17, that none of you or your offspring will be broke or be a sickling. For it is His will that you should prosper, be in good health, and in abundance. Speak John 10:10b, 1 Peter 2:24, and 3 John 2.

2 Peter 1:3-4, *"As His divine power has given to us all things that* pertain *to life and godliness, through the knowledge of Him who called us by glory and virtue, by which have been given to us exceedingly great and precious promises, that through these you may be partakers of the divine nature, having escaped the corruption* that is *in the world through lust."*

As you do this, allow the spirit of God to minister to you because situations might be different. There are some folks who are actually under a spell in their marriages. Some marriages are suffering from generational curses in their bloodlines. If there remain abnormal occurrences in the marriage, then I advise you to see a deliverance minister for counseling. For the Lord says in His Word that He will restore all the years that the locusts have eaten (Joel 2:25-26).

The Blessings of Job

Job 29:1-16 (commentary added),

"Job further continued his discourse, and said:

'Oh, that I were as in months past,

As in the days when God watched over me;
When His lamp shone upon my head,
And when by His light I walked through darkness;
Just as I was in the days of my prime,
When the friendly counsel of God was over my tent;
When the Almighty was yet with me,
When my children were around me;
[fruitfulness]
When my steps were bathed with cream,
And the rock poured out rivers of oil for me!
[prosperity]

'When I went out to the gate by the city,
When I took my seat in the open square,
The young men saw me and hid,
And the aged arose and stood;
The princes refrained from talking,
And put their hand on their mouth;
The voice of nobles was hushed,
And their tongue stuck to the roof of their mouth.
When the ear heard, then it blessed me,
And when the eye saw, then it approved me;
[high honor]
Because I delivered the poor who cried out,
The fatherless and the one who had no helper.

The blessing of a perishing man came upon me,
And I caused the widow's heart to sing for joy.
I put on righteousness, and it clothed me;
My justice was like a robe and a turban.
I was eyes to the blind,
And I was feet to the lame. [World changer]
I was a father to the poor,
And I searched out the case that I did not know."

Before Job was prosecuted by the devil for affliction as a result of his fears, he was a real blessing to his community. He was basking in the favor of the Lord. He was at the pinnacle of honor. He was a force to be reckoned with. These are the kinds of blessings that accompany the children of light when we live in the fear of the Lord.

Marriage is to Be Enjoyed

Proverb 5:15-19, *"Drink water from your own cistern, / And running water from your own well. / Should your fountains be dispersed abroad, / Streams of water in the streets? / Let them be only your own, / And not for strangers with you. / Let your fountain be blessed, / And rejoice with the*

wife of your youth. / As a loving deer and a graceful doe, / Let her breasts satisfy you at all times; / And always be enraptured with her love."

Marriage is not bondage. That is why God hates divorce. For when men divorce, we are indirectly saying to Him that marriage is not good. But He is never to be blamed. He did not put water in His mouth when He said it is good. The flesh and ignorance are the problems.

Song of Solomon 1:2-4, 12-16: *"[The Shulamite] Let him kiss me with the kisses of his mouth— / for your love is better than wine. / Because of the fragrance of your good ointments, / Your name is ointment poured forth; / Therefore the virgins love you. / Draw me away!*

"[The Daughters of Jerusalem] We will run after you.

"[The Shulamite] The king has brought me into his chambers.

"[The Daughters of Jerusalem] We will be glad and rejoice in you. / We will remember your love more than wine.

"[The Shulamite] Rightly do they love you ...

"[The Shulamite] While the king is *at his table, / My spikenard sends forth its fragrance. / A bundle of myrrh* is *my beloved to me, / That lies all night between my breasts. / My beloved* is *to me a cluster of henna* blooms */ In the vineyards of En Gedi.*

"[The Beloved] Behold, you are *fair, my love! / Behold, you* are *fair! / You* have *dove's eyes.*

"[The Shulamite] Behold, you are *handsome, my beloved! / Yes, pleasant! / Also our bed* is *green."*

Song of Solomon 7:11-13, "Come, my beloved, / Let us go forth to the field; / Let us lodge in the villages. / Let us get up early to the vineyards; / Let us see if the vine has budded, / Whether *the grape blossoms are open, /* And *the pomegranates are in bloom. / There I will give you my love. / The mandrakes give off a fragrance, / And at our gates* are *pleasant* fruits, */ All manner, new and old, / Which I have laid up for you, my beloved."*

They had quality time together. They went on vacations and went sightseeing, they ate good food, and they just enjoyed life. All these blessings can't be possible in abject, acute poverty or in the bed of sicknesses. This is what and how our Father wants us to enjoy our marriages. Legal and pure enjoyment is not a sin, and neither is it carnality.

A Poem of Love (Psalm 45:1-2, 8, 13-14)

"My heart is overflowing with a good theme;
I recite my composition concerning my King;
My tongue is the pen of a ready writer.

"You are fairer than the sons of men;
Grace is poured upon your lips;
Therefore God has blessed you forever ...

"All Your garments are scented with myrrh and aloes and cassia,
Out of the ivory palaces, by which they have made you glad ...

"The royal daughter is all glorious within the palace;
Her clothing is woven with gold.

"She shall be brought to the King in robes of many colors;
The virgins, her companions who follow her, because she kept herself, shall be brought to You."

With gladness and rejoicing the king shall embrace her and she shall be called a mother.

4

What is Marriage Then?

Marriage is a union between a man and a woman. It is a covenant of "into me see" between a mature male and a mature female. For God created them both—male and female—and He ordained that a man will leave his parents and join with his wife. Marriage unites two human beings in the most intimate and passionate relationship possible. These relationships have an intimacy and exclusiveness that can be found in no other relationship.

> **Genesis 2:24-25,** *"Therefore a man shall leave his father and mother and be joined to his wife, and they shall become one flesh.*
>
> *"And they were both naked, the man and his wife, and were not ashamed."*

Marriage is therefore not a relationship between people of the same sex group. Any union out of the above norm is against the standard laid and created by God. It is, therefore, an abomination (Leviticus 18:22 and 29, 20:13; Romans 1:26-32). Before the eyes of the creator, it is not marriage, and the partners will be punished by the Father if they do not repent or get out of it.

> **Leviticus 20:13, *"If a man lies with a male as he lies with a woman, both of them have committed an abomination. They shall surely be put to death. Their blood shall be upon them."***

When the Almighty God makes the rules and men break them because of rebellion and arrogance, they will pay dearly for it. It is not the will of God that any should perish. But whatever you sow, you shall reap.

Who Instituted Marriage?

Marriage was instituted by God because He did not want man to be alone. Marriage was not an idea from the devil. Marriage is God's idea. So, it is a good thing. And because God designed this institution, we have to ask Him to teach us the dynamics of marriage. Marriage is not for teenagers. So if you are a teenager, stay out of marriage for now, for marriage is far beyond the borders of sex. It was originally designed to be an antidote against human/physical loneliness. It is for those who are sick and tired of being lonely. It is not just about age, peer pressure, family pressure, sexual pressure, or any other pressures.

I say this because there are people who are single but who are not lonely enough. You should be ready to spend most of your time with your spouse. If you don't wish to do this or do not cherish their company enough, you will be heading toward a marital disaster. Marriage is to be enjoyed and not to be endured. There are some folks who spend most of their time with other folks rather than with their spouse. Please do not go into marriage if you are not ready to spend the majority of your time with your spouse. If you still have other bodies to hang out with and spend most of your time with, please do not go into the institution of marriage. This union, like I said before, is more than just sex. Therefore, there is a lot of sex going on but very few to commit to marriage. No wonder all those babies are born out of wedlock. Sex does not need any serious preparation.

What is not marriage?

> Marriage is not co-habitation. If you are living together and enjoying the benefits apportioned to marriage only without a

public commitment, then you are living in sin.

➤ Marriage is not between two people of the same sex.

➤ Marriage is not a boyfriend or girlfriend relationship.

➤ Marriage is not the so-called common law marriage. Even though one has the intention to be married to another, they both can't live together as if they are married. Wearing a ring on your finger, filing taxes jointly, or taking someone's last name does not fulfill God's standard of marriage.

To add to this, wearing a ring on the fourth finger on your left hand is not what marriage is all about. In fact, as true children of God, we are to follow the Word of God and not the traditions of this world.

There is no marriage ring mentioned in the Bible, anywhere, from Genesis to Revelation. And God never told us to put one on. He did not put one on the first couples. A MARRIAGE RING IS NOT BIBLICAL. It is all part of paganistic ornamentations. It is one of those things that was introduced to true Christianity by pagans. ANCIENT ROME CAUSED SO MUCH HAVOC TO THE GOSPEL AND DISTORTIONS TO SCRIPTURES. Many professing Christians will fail

God's judgment in this area. For in the beginning, it was not so. They can't show HIM in the same Bible they carry and believe in. Whatever we do in or on this body, we should be ready to give an account of it to the one who will judge us.

> **2 Corinthians 5:10,** *"For we must all appear before the judgment seat of Christ, that each one may receive the things done in the body, according to what he has done, whether good or bad."*

> **Revelation 20:12-13,** *"And I saw the dead, small and great, standing before God, and books were opened. And another book was opened, which is the Book of Life. And the dead were judged according to their works, by the things which were written in the books.*

> *The sea gave up the dead who were in it, and Death and Hades delivered up the dead who were in them. And they were judged, each one according to his works."*

There shall be judgments, and the judgments are related to the things we did. The route of escape from the one in Revelation is to truly repent and be converted.

Acts 3:19, *"Repent therefore and be converted, that your sins may be blotted out, so that times of refreshing may come from the presence of the Lord."*

➤ Marriage is not between humans and spirits.
➤ Marriage is not between humans and animals.
➤ Marriage is not a contract. It is a covenant.
➤ Marriage is marriage when it is of God's standard.

The differences between sex and marriage:

Marriage	Sex
Intense preparations	No intense preparations
Parents must give consent	No parental permission needed
For life	Short term
Serious commitment	No commitment necessary
Driven by love	Driven by lust
Can't be spontaneous	Can happen instantly

Marriage is Honorable

The hunger or longing for companionship is what will keep the marriage strong—not just sex alone. There are many married couples who will attest that this is true. Please, if you are not lonely enough, don't go into marriage, because you will ruin someone else's joy.

Genesis 2:20-21.

If you still have a sugar daddy or sugar babes around you and with you, then you will not be able to enter into God's perfect will until you get rid of them.

Marriage is very important to society. A better marriage means a better family. And better families build a better society. A messed-up marriage leads to a disorganized, disoriented, deformed and dysfunctional society. That is why the devil's attack on the first marriage in the garden of Eden has left the whole world living in a disaster. The failure of the first couples brought the world to the sufferings we are experiencing today. If we can get our marital homes straight, there will be fewer drug addicts, less prostitution, and fewer gangsters, crimes, etc. So please, do not rush into this institution impromptu because that will ruin your life and the seeds after you.

5

ATM

Abstinence Till Marriage

The Word of God encourages us to be holy, for God is holy. Holiness is not a must. It must not be a burden to us.

> **1 John 5:3,** *"For this is the love of God, that we keep His commandments. And His commandments are not burdensome."*

> **1 Peter 1:15-19,** *"But as He who called you is **holy, you also be holy in all** your **conduct, because it is written, 'Be holy, for I am holy'.**

> *"And if you call on the Father, who without partiality judges according to each one's work, conduct yourselves throughout the time of your stay here in fear; knowing that you were not redeemed with corruptible things, like silver or gold, from your aimless*

conduct received *by tradition from your fathers, but with the precious blood of Christ, as of a lamb without blemish and without spot."*

God is not forcing this on us. He is not a dictator. He wants us to walk in love (John 14:23). When we operate in love toward our Father, His commandments will not be burdensome to us. He already knows the consequences of when we disobey. Yes, He is the God of forgiveness, mercies, and compassion. But there are consequences of sin that can't be stopped by any man. For example, the sin in the garden of Eden was forgiven, but man can't be immortal anymore.

Child of God, let not the passing pleasures of sin or of this world take away from you God's destiny for your life. For our body is the temple of the Holy Ghost. It can't be defiled. Simply obey what the Lord is saying and keep yourself pure before marriage. Remember, the sin will be forgiven but the consequences will ruin your life, take away your joy, and leave you in a place of regrets. For example, some people right now are lamenting under the consequences of personal sins that have already been forgiven. But even though this sin was forgiven, some folks can't get married as planned because one venereal or terminal disease is eating them up. Some of you have repented, but your spiritual husband or wife can't allow you to marry. They are still harassing you. Even though you have repented, you were incarcerated. Yes, you repented, but there was a divorce. And the guilt and the shame are still your worst nightmare. Though the Lord Jesus has the power to heal, deliver, and set free, prevention is better than cure. It is good to stay away from those sins that easily besiege us.

> **Hebrews 12:1-4,** *"Therefore we also, since we are surrounded by so great a cloud of witnesses, let us lay aside every weight, and the sin which so easily ensnares us, and let us run with endurance the race that is set before us, looking unto Jesus, the author and finisher of our faith, who for the joy that was set before Him endured the cross, despising the shame, and has sat down at the right hand of the throne of God.*
>
> *"For consider Him who endured such hostility from sinners against Himself, lest you become weary and discouraged in your souls. You have not yet resisted to bloodshed, striving against sin."*

Those of you who have already been through these experiences, please advise the younger ones so that they will not become prey for the enemy. If you are a youth or someone who is getting ready to initiate a sexual relationship with someone you are not married to, or before marriage, please don't.

Job 17:9, *"Yet the righteous will hold to his way, / And he who has clean hands will be stronger and stronger."*

Friends may mock you or laugh at you right now for not indulging in sin, but they will appreciate you and learn from you later. You will have the final say.

How to maintain your ATM card

A. Spend quality time with the Word of God (Psalm 119:9, 11, 67). You see, if you spend time with His Word, it will become what I call a LAFE (**la**mp unto my **fe**et) and a LIPA (**li**ght unto my **pa**th).

Psalm 119:9, *"How can a young man cleanse his way? / By taking heed according to Your word."*

B. Develop and cultivate a lifestyle of prayer and fasting. You can't give yourself all the satisfaction of the flesh and expect to overcome all the temptations of the flesh. Do not forget that flesh is flesh, a woman is a woman, and a man is a man. The eye of the flesh does not discriminate for who is born again or not. Not at all! That guy (sex organ) does not discriminate. Positive and negative will always attract. Our flesh is not born again, neither is it spiritual. It is still the same old flesh you have always had. Therefore, we can't afford to allow him to go operating unchecked. We need to take authority and be in control. If not, there will be a knock at the door one day, and you will be in the wrong place.

Proverbs 6:27-28, *"Can a man take fire to his bosom, / And his clothes not be burned? / Can one walk on hot coals, / And his feet not be seared?"*

1 John 2:16-17, *"For all that is in the world—the lust of the flesh, the lust of the eyes, and the pride of life—is not of the Father but is of the world. And the world is passing away, and the lust of it; but he who does the will of God abides forever."*

Galatians 5:16-17, *"I say then: Walk in the Spirit, and you shall not fulfill the lust of the flesh. For the flesh lusts against the Spirit, and the Spirit against the flesh; and these are contrary to one another, so that you do not do the things that you wish."*

Fasting with prayer and the Word of God will give your spirit man dominion, pre-eminence, authority, and control over your flesh.

Check these passages out: Mark 14:38, 9:28-29; Luke 6:12.

Please do not say you can't fast. If you are really determined to maintain ATM, you will find yourself in the flow. Fasting is simply abstaining from physical nourishment so that you can spend quality time with God. Simply eat no food and go after God. The Lord Jesus, our role model, was a man of prayer and fasting. The apostle Paul lived a lifestyle of fasting.

2 Corinthians 11:27, *"In weariness and toil, in sleeplessness often, in hunger and thirst, in fastings often, in cold and nakedness."*

Luke 6:12, *"Now it came to pass in those days that He went out to the mountain to pray, and continued all night in prayer to God."*

C. Our companionship: (1 Corinthians 6:17, James 4:4-8) We are joined to the Lord when we invite Him to come into our lives. And when we draw close to Him, He will draw close to us. And when He comes, He will come with His attributes. The more of Him we have, the less trouble we have fighting with the flesh. Living the Word and spending quality time with the Lord in prayer and fasting will cause the fear of God to be stronger in us and will strengthen our love for Him. These will help us to stay holy:

i. To flee sexual immorality and fornication

ii. To be determined to enter holy matrimony as a virgin, despite all odds

iii. To choose who our friends are and who to hang out with

iv. Not to go to places that will depress your spirit and that will feed your flesh and stir up the desire of the old man. Instead, decide to be active in church.

When we draw nearer to God:

➤ He will order our steps.

➤ He will help us to know who and what will edify us.

➤ His spirit in us will not allow us to watch certain movies, to glance through inappropriate magazines, or to listen to ungodly brands of music.

If you love Him, you will also love to have fellowship with Him.

Job 15:34, *"For the company of hypocrites will be barren, / And fire will consume the tents of bribery."*

ATM versus Compromise

Compromise is the devil's instrument to the ATM overdraft: refuse to sell your self-esteem and integrity to compromise. Do not go after the God of the uncircumcised Philistines. His name is Compromise. So many mighty men have lost their position with God because of him. Do not sell your birthright to Mr. Compromise, because he will not give it back to you. Compromise is a swine. If you cast your pearls to him, he will trample on them. Compromise wants you to dance the idolatrous dance of the Egyptians, so that God can spank you as He did with the men in the wilderness. Say NO to compromise and YES to ATM. Choose abstinence over compromise. The sin of compromising has cost the lives of people who could not zip up. Some ended up in jails, some ended up in divorce, some are in the hospital, and some ended up in their graves. For others, their careers or educational paths were ruined. Others lost their jobs, and their business partners walked away. Some were forced to let go of their kids, while others decided to commit suicide. And because of Mr. Compromise, others ended up with unwanted pregnancies, committed abortions, and many became single parents.

ATM (abstinence till marriage) should be your best friend, role model, and the vehicle to ride in on the journey toward marriage. ATM is the only antidote, defense, and security against compromise.

Proverbs 4:8-10, *"'Exalt her, and she will promote you; / She will bring you honor, when you embrace her. / She will place on your head an ornament of grace; / A crown of glory she will deliver to you.' / Hear, my son, and receive my sayings, and the years of your life will be many."*

Remember Joseph in the Bible.

6

Virgins wanted!

Virgins Wanted is the cry of ATM (Abstinence Till Marriage). In Esther 2:2, young virgins were sought for an earthly king. King Ahasuerus, with the help of his servants, decided to look for a wife after Queen Vashti messed up. Now there were so many young ladies around, but only virgins were allowed to compete or run for the pageant. Now the question is, If an earthly king needed a virgin, do you think our heavenly Father would go for anything less? Child of God, there is power in your virginity! It will take you to places and open doors that would not have been opened by any other means. Before God, you will be highly esteemed above your counterparts. So endeavor to keep your heart and body holy. This will help you to not attract the wrong personalities into your life. My advice to you: clothe yourself decently.

Esther 2:1-3, *"After these things, when the wrath of King Ahasuerus subsided, he remembered Vashti, what she had done, and what had been decreed against her. Then the king's servants who attended him said: 'Let beautiful young virgins be sought for the king; and let the king appoint officers in all the provinces of his kingdom, that they may gather all the beautiful young virgins to Shushan the citadel, into the women's quarters, under the custody of Hegai the king's eunuch, custodian of the women. And let beauty preparations be given them.'"*

Just so you know, the above setting was from people who were in darkness. The decision was rooted in pride. It had nothing to do with God. These people were not worshippers of the God of Israel (The God of Holiness).

Today, we as spiritual people are not led by flesh. The flesh is not our teacher (Galatians 5:16, Romans 8:14). This is what pagans do best. They operate by their flesh. They work by sight. We are supposed to circumcise the flesh from being our guide.

Colossians 2:11, *"In Him you were also circumcised with the circumcision made without hands, by putting off the body of* *the sins of the flesh, by the circumcision of Christ."*

Kill it by obeying the Word of God. GOD'S children are to walk in the spirit. Be led by the Spirit. Walk in faith. Nothing that is fleshly pleases our own king in heaven. No flesh is allowed to glory in HIS presence.1 Corinthians 1:29).

Today, the beauty preparation needed to be done in order for us to be accepted by the king in heaven or to see His face is holiness (Hebrew 12:14, Psalm 29:3). And this holiness is inward and outward, as it was with Adam and Eve before the paganistic methods and lifestyles were introduced by the devil.

2 Corinthians 7:1, *"Therefore, having these promises, beloved, let us cleanse ourselves from all filthiness of the flesh and spirit, perfecting holiness in the fear of God."*

GOING BACK TO OUR ORIGINAL NATURE INSIDE AND OUTSIDE IS WHAT JESUS MEANT BY "UNLESS A MAN IS BORN AGAIN." Nothing less! We must go back to a place of complete obedience and be totally void of anything that was not there in the beginning with our first parents.

Oh dear, there are a lot of things we are doing to ourselves or in us that in the beginning were not so. WHILE MEN SLEPT AND WHILE THE CHURCH SLEPT, THE ENEMY CAME AND SOWED TARES. WHO HAS DONE THIS?

The Bible answers: an enemy (Matthew 13:25-30).

Some of you are about to put on ungodly attire on your wedding day.

Proverbs 7:10, "*And there a woman met him, With the attire of a harlot, and a crafty heart.*"

PROSTITUTES' ATTIRES DO NOT COVER THE BODY. These are dresses or fashions that reveal your nakedness. They expose sensitive parts of your body. Do not give others a wrong impression or a wrong image about yourself. Do not send the wrong message. This is where fig leaves were introduced to humans. **Genesis 3:7, "*Then the eyes of both of them were opened,*"**

*and they knew that they were naked;
and they sewed fig leaves together and
made themselves coverings.*" Your body is
supposed to be well-clothed. It is the temple
of God.

1 Corinthians 6:19, *"Or do you not know
that your body is the temple of the Holy
Spirit who is in you, whom you have from
God, and you are not your own?"*

Any man that defiles the temple of God will
be thrown into hell if they don't repent.

1 Corinthians 3:17, *"If anyone defiles the
temple of God, God will destroy him. For
the temple of God is holy, which temple you
are."*

God will not excuse you, even on your
wedding day. Be warned! This is not a popular
message. And this is one of the reasons
that many church people are going to hell,
including their preachers.

Matthew 7:22-23, *"Many will say to Me
in that day, 'Lord, Lord, have we not
prophesied in Your name, cast out demons
in Your name, and done many wonders
in Your name?' And then I will declare to*

them, 'I never knew you; depart from Me, you who practice lawlessness!'"

You see, those preachers were sent by the Lord to hell. They only wanted members or money or prestige. They tell you, "God sees the heart." Fine! But men look at your body, and out of that same heart proceeds all the thoughts to dress sexually. What about people defiling the temple of God? Fear God. Not men's standard or popular trends. We can't lower HIM into our level of holiness!

Matthew 5:28, *"But I say to you that whoever looks at a woman to lust for her has already committed adultery with her in his heart."*

Yes, some will still fall. But you can do your part to escape the judgment of God.

1 Corinthians 8:9, *"But beware lest somehow this liberty of yours become a stumbling block to those who are weak."*

Contact us for more in-depth scriptural insights. Do not follow the crowd. **Exodus 23:2,** *"You shall not follow a crowd to do evil; nor shall you testify in a dispute so as to turn aside after many to pervert justice."*

Save yourself from this untoward church generation (Acts 2:40). In the beginning, it was not so.

Some of you will pay huge amounts of money to makeup artists to redesign your lips, eyebrows, nails, and so on. That is a mockery and an insult to God (Psalm 139:13-14). Your discontentment has made you ungodly (Romans 1:18, 1 Timothy 6:6). Some will call it a face lift. This is evil and against God's perfect work (Genesis 1:31).

In the beginning, it was not so! The Lord will not allow such people to enter His heaven if they don't repent. These are just some of the things that pagans do. And paganism is a sin (1 Peter 4:2-3).

For the above practice is falsehood and is a lie. For example, the eyebrows are fake. The nails are not yours. You are all too artificial. None is original. None telleth the truth to the other. These are all lying Christians. THEY LIE WTH THEIR APPEARANCES. HELL IS ONLY LOOKING FOR ONE SIN (Ephesians 5:27).

We know the end result.

Revelation 21:8, *"But the cowardly, unbelieving, abominable, murderers, sexually immoral, sorcerers, idolaters, and all liars shall have their part in the lake which burns with fire and brimstone, which is the second death."*

This is a good reason not to lie.

Revelation 22:15 (KJV), *"For without are dogs, and sorcerers, and whoremongers, and murderers, and idolaters, and whosoever loveth and maketh a lie."*

Luke 14:26, *"If anyone comes to Me and does not hate his father and mother, wife and children, brothers and sisters, yes, and his own life also, he cannot be My disciple."*

AND MY PEOPLE LOVE IT SO (Jeremiah 5:31).

Therefore, the Lord Jesus said do not allow the lust or the cravings of the members of your body (eyebrows, lips, nails, etc.) make you miss heaven. Cut this practice off! Stop it! Discipline your flesh! We should kill the discontentment and our covetous nature. Some of you will even go as far as bleaching your bodies.

Matthew 5:29-30, *"If your right eye causes you to sin, pluck it out and cast it from you; for it is more profitable for you that one of your members perish, than for your whole body to be cast into hell. And if your right hand causes you to sin, cut it off and cast it from you; for it is more profitable for you that one of your members perish, than for your whole body to be cast into hell."*

Why is all this happening? A lack of knowledge means that God's people are perishing. IGNORANCE IS NOT AN EXCUSE IN THE COURT OF LAW. Please don't be angry. We did it also. I have been there and done that. We have all been blind. If the trumpet would have sounded on my wedding day, I would have been the man most miserable of all. But God later revealed this truth to me.

God has done His part to bring men out of the darkness of paganism (1 John 5:19, 3:8-9). But you see, it is men who loved the darkness of the Adamic nature. The love for darkness is in our nature (John 3:19). That is why most of God's temples today are filled with junk. Men love it that way. And they call it church (Jeremiah 2:3). No wonder the Lord spoke to us through a revelation: **"My church is** dirty." Therefore, the Bible is admonishing us to crucify our inherited sinful nature and flesh and put on the new man (Ephesians 4:19-25, 5:8), by going to the cross, through the cross, and carrying the cross.

NO CROSS, NO HEAVEN.

We can't be followers of Christ without our own cross (Luke 14:27). It was impressed upon my spirit some months ago to also carry my own cross and allow myself to be crucified on it just like my master. The life of the cross is the life of separation from the pattern of this present evil world (James 4:4, 1 John 2:16-17, 2 Timothy 4:10).

Let's continue talking about virgins wanted.
When God was ready to send His son into the world, He went after a virgin. Virgins are powerful tools in the hands of God because of their purity. Even occultists understand this secret. Therefore in their kingdom, virgins are in high demand. They commit all types of sexual atrocities, and most especially they go after virgins. Their preachers (in churches) are mostly involved in sexual misconduct. In the kingdom of darkness, sexual immorality is the greatest weapon against humanity. In the realm of the spirit, when the powers of darkness use virgins, the results are inevitable

(e.g. children in witchcraft, adults having intercourse with young boys and girls, etc.).

A child of God who is a virgin (especially an intercessor) is extremely dangerous in the realm of the spirit. Therefore, run away! Run away from illicit sex. It is dangerous. It might cost you your life.

God is looking for virgins. Virgins also are God's best. Some years ago, He came through a virgin into the world. Her name was Mary, but today we call her Virgin Mary. Young friends, even if you think you can't do anything for God in terms of giftings or calling, just live your life as a virgin and your name shall be in God's book of remembrance. Who said virginity availed nothing? This is a big lie. KEEP YOURSELF TIED. Zip up! And never let loose until God releases you. Joseph's virgin was made a mother of Israel right before her peers. For those of you who worship or pray through Mary, you are missing the point. You need to learn from her. Use her as your reason to remain a virgin. Let Mama Mary be the driving force to keep you from distractors. You cannot be calling yourself cadets of Mary, daughters of Mary, children of Mary, or sisters of Mary if you're messing around. If you are living such a life, then you are deceiving yourself because Mama Mary will not save you. What Mama Mary and the Lord Jesus require from you is following or imitating that lifestyle that made the Almighty choose her. Mama Mary is not the pinnacle of worship, but her lifestyle should be copied by young believers.

There are so many daughters of Mary who are bringing tears to her eyes. Yes, they are causing her to shed tears because when she watches them amongst the great clouds of witness in heaven, she weeps over their adulterous and fornicating lifestyles. She will be incredibly happy if you repent today. Her son Jesus is always very ready to forgive you. It will do you and Mama Mary no good if you are following her and you are not living the lifestyle she expects from you.

Virgins before the Lord are like a sacrifice without spot and blemish. The LORD JESUS is coming for a virgin church/bride (2 Corinthians 11:2).

1 Peter 1:17-19, *"And if you call on the Father, who without partiality judges according to each one's work, conduct yourselves throughout the time of your stay here in fear; knowing that you were*

not redeemed with corruptible things, like
silver or gold, from your aimless conduct
received *by tradition from your fathers,
but with the precious blood of Christ, as of
a lamb without blemish and without spot."*

That is why they are God's best. He went
after the virgin daughter of Jephthah as a
fulfillment of his vow.

Judges 11:30-39, *"And Jephthah made a
vow to the LORD, and said, 'If You will
indeed deliver the people of Ammon into
my hands, then it will be that whatever
comes out of the doors of my house to meet
me, when I return in peace from the people
of Ammon, shall surely be the LORD's, and
I will offer it up as a burnt offering.'*

*"So Jephthah advanced toward the people
of Ammon to fight against them, and the
LORD delivered them into his hands.
And he defeated them from Aroer as far
as Minnith—twenty cities—and to Abel
Keramim, with a very great slaughter. Thus
the people of Ammon were subdued before
the children of Israel.*

*"When Jephthah came to his house at
Mizpah, there his daughter, coming*

out to meet him with timbrels and dancing; and she was his *only child. Besides her he had neither son nor daughter. And it came to pass, when he saw her, that he tore his clothes, and said, 'Alas, my daughter! You have brought me very low! You are among those who trouble me! For I have given my word to the LORD, and I cannot go back on it.'*

"So she said to him, 'My father, if you have given your word to the LORD, do to me according to what has gone out of your mouth, because the LORD has avenged you of your enemies, the people of Ammon.' Then she said to her father, 'Let this thing be done for me: let me alone for two months, that I may go and wander on the mountains and bewail my virginity, my friends and I.'

"So he said, 'Go.' And he sent her away for two months; and she went with her friends, and bewailed her virginity on the mountains. And it was so at the end of two months that she returned to her father, and he carried out his vow with her which he had vowed. She knew no man.

"And it became a custom in Israel."

I personally believe it was not because she was his only child but because she was a virgin. This is because the Lord wanted a sacrifice without spot or blemish, and his daughter was the only option He could lay His hands on. Once again, the Lord was looking for virgins. They are precious instruments and highly effective in the spirit realm. They are a very costly sacrifice, especially if you have only one. Jephthah was probably not happy at all, but he had to fulfill his vow.

When King David was old and sick and needed a caregiver, they did not just look for any woman for the old man. In our days, the people would have said "a woman is a woman," but they went searching for a virgin. The king wanted a virgin. It was a shock, especially to his children. He should have gotten someone who had the experience already on how to take care of an old man. I think he wanted someone who would not have ulterior motives. He did not need somebody who would kill him quickly. He needed someone whose eyes had not opened yet. He needed someone who would be there for him and not for what he had. He needed someone without spot or blemish. But most of the folks around him did not understand. Now I know why his son Solomon made this statement.

Proverb 30:18-19 (emphasis added), *"There are three things which are too wonderful for me, / Yes, four which I do not understand: / The way of an eagle in the air, / The way of a serpent on a rock, / The way of a ship in the midst of the sea, / And the way of a man with a virgin."*

But number four he did not understand. Keep yourself precious and keep your ATM card. That is your "joke" card. Don't allow anybody (male or female) to mess with you. For one of these days, the king will come looking for you. It will happen in the twinkling of an eye. I see the Lord coming for you. You are about to celebrate your virginity in grand style. Don't be hasty. Do not offer yourself to the slaughterers before your time. Don't allow those boys, those girls, to fool you. Stand still. Take a deep breath. Relax. Don't move, and don't take any steps further. I see the prince getting ready. He will be there shortly with the king. Do not sell your virginity for a pot of soup. Life is more than all that talk and hype. Finish your race. Go for the crown. Go for the trophy.

Hebrews 12:1, *"Therefore we also, since we are surrounded by so great a cloud of* *witnesses, let us lay aside every weight, and the sin which so easily ensnares* us, *and let us run with endurance the race that is set before us."*

Hebrews 4:15, *"For we do not have a High Priest who cannot sympathize with our weaknesses, but was in all points tempted as we are, yet without sin."*

➤ Sons and daughters of Zion, keep yourselves for the best because the king's servants and the world are watching. Remember, even if your peers have derailed from the master's plan, be determined to be a pacesetter. It is not about how fast you run but how well you finish. Joseph went back to the palace because he decided to keep ATM. He became the governor of a foreign land because of his firm belief in ATM. Do not delay that which God has pre-destined for your life by derailing yourself because of the flesh. The Lord loves using pure, youthful vessels, e.g. David, Joseph, Jeremiah, Samuel, etc. The Lord takes pleasure in people who are young and pure. Wait upon the Lord and again I say wait. Let us offer our body as a living sacrifice unto the master.

Spiritual Virgins

These are those who became virgins through **2 Corinthians 5:17:** *"Therefore, if anyone is in Christ, he is a new creation; old things have passed away; behold, all things have become new."*

In the eyes of God and in the realm of the spirit, you are equally a powerful tool in the hands of the master. Only you must make sure you do not return to your old life. The enemy is eyeing you up big time. He will always replay those old days in the hopes of whetting your appetite to get you to renounce your virginity. Whether you are a natural virgin or a spiritual virgin, do not sell your birthright. The devil is busy going back and forth looking for precious ones like you to put down. Do not fall for him. Quickly put up your N.C.N.F.S sign (not cheap, no fishing, not for sale).

Please do not go back to your vomit. Pull and hold it through until that faithful day. You can padlock it and bring the key to the Lord Jesus. For He is able to keep you from falling. The grand opening (the wedding day) is the only trigger to get the key out.

The Danger and the Consequences of a Broken Vow of ATM

1 Corinthians 6:18, *"Flee sexual immorality. Every sin that a man does is outside the body, but he who commits sexual immorality sins against his own body."*

It says flee, because if you don't, you will end up in a **blood covenant**. This will legally permit spiritual husbands and wives to torment you. (These are beings that have sex with some folks while they sleep. In some cases, they will prevent them from marrying in this physical world.) This covenant will only be broken and be made void through the Lord JESUS. Deliverance by the Lord Jesus is the only way out when you are bombarded with things and by things that you can't control. If the covenant is not dealt with, it will move from one generation to another. Some people end up with broken marriages, barrenness, divorce, promiscuity, miscarriages, infidelity, singleness, terminal illnesses, venereal diseases, and continual harassment from the powers of darkness.

You will also destroy God's shields of protection around you because of disobedience (Proverbs

5:15-18). You have rebelled; you have broken God's order. If you initiate it, you will also pay the price.

> **Proverbs 6:27-28,** ***"Can a man take fire to his bosom,***
> ***And his clothes not be burned?***
> ***Can one walk on hot coals,***
> ***And his feet not be seared?"***

You will also find yourself in a deep pit (Proverbs 23:27-28). The disobedience of God's order will lead to death and hell if repentance is not quickly carried out.

> **Proverbs 5:3-5,** ***"For the lips of an immoral woman drip honey,***
> ***And her mouth is smoother than oil;***
> ***But in the end she is bitter as wormwood,***
> ***Sharp as a two-edged sword.***
> ***Her feet go down to death,***
> ***Her steps lay hold of hell."***

Guys, do not be wise in your own eyes (Proverbs 5:21, 3:7).

Do not be deceived by the saying, "We can control it; we can use pills, condoms, etc." What if the system fails? Of course, it has happened over and over again. There is no safe period, and there is no safe method except ATM. The one who created your body can cause failures in those techniques—abnormalities, impossibilities, and mysteries. God can do the impossible every now and then. It happened with Sarah and Abraham, Jonah in the fish's belly, the birth of Christ, and many more.

The day the creator decides to take it no more (in reference to our context), the consequences will be abortion, unwanted pregnancy, venereal diseases, HIV, etc. By the way, AIDS is a killing disease because man decided to disobey God. The Lord knew the consequences of sexual immorality even before we were born. Therefore, He began warning His people in the days of old not to indulge in the act. But men loved darkness and they decided to ignore Him, and the rest of the story today is pathetic. When the Lord forbids us from doing something, it is for our good. For God is not mocked; whatever we sow we shall reap.

Galatians 6:7-8, *"Do not be deceived, God is not mocked; for whatever a man sows, that he will also reap. For he who sows to his flesh will of the flesh reap corruption, but he who sows to the Spirit will of the Spirit reap everlasting life."*

Therefore, he who has ears, let them hear. Do not harden your heart. For God is not a respecter of persons. For people perish for lack of knowledge. Buy the truth and sell it not. And you will know the truth and the truth you know will set you free.

Also, having too many partners before marriage can cause problems down the line in your marriage. Some characteristics of some **old soul ties** can become a constant nightmare in your marriage. It will not be a good sight to behold when such imaginations and fantasies besiege your spouse. Will you like to deal with so many spiritual or physical Johnnies and Suzies after your wedding? My people say, "E better no be" (it will not be cool).

This can lead to abortion due to **unwanted pregnancy**. And repeated abortions can cause pelvic infections, which can lead to infertility.

When girls start having sex at an early age, it is more likely they will be exposed to sexually transmitted diseases, thus **risking fertility**. Sexually transmitted diseases will later infect their spouse and children if they are not discovered early.

7

Supplement: My Advice While You Wait

Serve the Lord now with all the strength you have. If you can't be more committed when you are single, then when you get married you may find it difficult to really commit. Singles who give a lot of excuses why they can't be regular in church activities will give more excuses when they get married. I speak this out of experience, not as a doctrine (1 Corinthians 7). Give your all now that you are single, and when you get married, strive to maintain that same commitment. Remember that God sees the heart and knows exactly what we are up to.

God is still merciful. Some of you may have mistaken God's will when it was time to marry, but God is still merciful. Some of you were moved by sight and emotion when a prospect came and you did not really wait on the Lord to open your eyes. If you made that mistake, don't be too mad at yourself. For God is still merciful. Plead with Him for mercy. Some of you also actually turned your back on God's chosen because you were also moved by the same emotion and were not patient enough to wait on the Lord. The bottom line is to be sensitive to the intuition of the Holy Ghost in order not to miss divine visitation or vice versa. You want to marry a wife and not a knife, a husband and not a horseman, a wife and not a witch, a husband and not house bondage. The person you marry can either become a barrier or a breakthrough.

Love is a decision. It might not be felt in the first instance and may not even have attraction.

While you wait, make every effort to get good materials and attend seminars and meetings that prepare you for marriage. Do not wait until you find someone or get a proposal. Marriage is the only institution whereby the learning curve never stops.

Get rid of any bitterness. Forgive those who hurt you, whether directly or indirectly. Forgive yourself. Seek peace and reconciliation. Do not harbor what they did wrong to you. Unforgiveness and bitterness can shut marital doors for the longest time.

Do not try to play games with prospects or potential prospects. As soon as you hear from heaven, let your yes be yes or your no be no. Don't be lingering around. You are inviting the devil without knowing. The undesirable happens when he takes up a case. Some folks end up being cursed.

Dress the way you want to be addressed. Do not invite the wrong prospects by your style of dressing.

Seek deliverance or counseling if abnormal phenomena keep on reoccurring. For example, frequent break-ups for no righteous reason.

What do you do when you find the right prospect?

Take them to your spiritual leader. He or she will tell you the right things to do.

They will help to pray also. With two or three witnesses, a special thing can be established. But make sure your leader is genuine.

Lies from hell to singles

> You will just blow it; therefore, nobody will marry you again.

➤ You are too dark, too skinny, too fat, too short.

➤ In this 21ˢᵗ century, people do not marry uncultivated, uneducated villagers like you.

➤ Younger babes won't give you a chance.

➤ Young women do not marry old men like you.

➤ Your biological clock is soon running out. Even if you get married, you will not produce children.

➤ Marriage is not for you. Forget it. Just curse God about your situation.

Do not believe all these lies and the many more you will be told. There is a man for every woman. The Lord who instituted marriage knew it is not good to be alone. When He said it is not good, He did not put water in His mouth. He meant what He said. If we seek Him diligently, we will find Him. He is the rewarder of those who diligently seek Him. Even if your case has been written off by men, He has a spouse for you. All you need to do is to be determined to wait on God's perfect will. And if that perfect will means that you will serve HIM as a single person, you will be very peaceful (1 Corinthians 7:7-8).

When you seek Him diligently, that is real faith. And faith rewards those who seek Him untiringly. When you do this, He has only one choice—to come down. And when He does, He will show you the problem and how to solve it, or He will give you the solution. He reveals to redeem. Therefore, do not believe all these lies from the devil. He is the accuser of the brethren. Just make sure that you do not owe him anything. If you do, you must plead with God, confess, renounce, and cancel. The Lord is still merciful. For many are the afflictions (attacks, sufferings, pains) of the righteous, but the Lord will deliver them from all (Ps.34:19).

Before and after you get married

1. Let the zeal and the passion for holy living be stronger.

2. Let the zeal and passion for the Lord's work consume you the most.

3. Be slow to speak and don't be a fault finder.

4. Treat each other with respect.

5. Always remember that marriage is not the end of your Christianity. HEAVEN IS THE GOAL. Do not enter into compromising.

6. If you are willing and determined to enter heaven by fire or by thunder or come whatever, then you will not fail.

7. Heaven is the limit. The devil is defeated. And JESUS is up and up and never down!

During the time of courtship

1. Make sure you are accountable: every place you go or things you do between each other or around each other must be in the light. Nothing should be done in darkness. Get some trusted brethren or leadership involved. Let them be aware of your moves. This will help you avoid every appearance of evil and keep your garments spotless. Do not think you are too spiritual to handle Mr. Flesh. Any man that thinketh, he stands lest he fall (1 Corinthians 10:12). I speak the truth in Christ. It is the most tempting part in this whole marriage process. I have been through this. So, I'm telling y'all, don't joke with flesh.

2. Be transparent: do not cover any evil. Make sure you tell them any secrets before they find out.

3. Background checks: do intensive, detailed, in-depth checks on his/her family, spiritual life, financial life, marital life (if he was married before, does he/she have children, are they divorced, sex life, etc.). Do not take this lightly. You have the right to understand and to know what you are getting into. Marriage is for life. You can't get in and get out the next day. Do your due diligence

so that when you say "I do," you know what (at least humanly) you are agreeing to. Do not be carried away by emotions. They are seasonal. Get knowledge and get understanding. It will keep you married. Marriage can either make you or break you. It can take you to heaven or hell. It can be heaven on earth or hell. So, take it seriously. It can't be trial by error. If you don't understand anything, ask again and again until you do. Also, if you read this material thus far and you think you are not ready, then put off the marriage idea and get proper knowledge and counseling. Do not go in with an unstable heart. Be convinced of your decision. Why should you die a common death?

4. Get acquainted with the parents or immediate family of your spouse-to-be. Know who they are at least. This is a wise thing to do.

Suggestion before the wedding day

Set a time to pray through the wedding process. The enemy is not happy seeing you fulfilling God's plan. He will do anything to mess up your happiness. Make sure you pray him out before he surprises you with unwanted guests such as car failures, bad weather conditions, demonic traffic jams, servers or workers being attacked, etc. For example, on my wedding day, our DJ was arrested mysteriously by police early in the morning. It took divine intervention for him to be released. And, amazingly, he was one of the very first to get to the reception location. I was shocked when he told me he was just coming from the police station.

No sex before the wedding if you plan to have one.

Before you say "Yes, I do," then make sure you know the vision of your spouse and the purpose of the union. If the marriage does not have a vision, then it does not have an eye. NO EYE MEANS IT CAN GO IN ANY DIRECTION, AND IT BEING ABLE TO GO IN ANY DIRECTION MEANS THAT THERE WILL ALWAYS BE TROUBLE. PEOPLE WHO ARE NOT ON A MISSION WILL BE DISTRACTED BY ANY LITTLE THING, WHICH WILL DEFINITELY BRING COMMOTION INTO THE UNION. Ask yourself the question, "Why are we coming together? What is the purpose we are to accomplish?" If carefulness is not paid to this question, many become lukewarm in the things of God after marriage. THEY NOW HAVE WHAT THEY WANTED: MARRIAGE, NOT MARRIAGE TO FULFILL A MISSION.

Prayer points

> Lord, forgive me for any sin.

➤ Lord, give me the grace to forgive anyone that has hurt me in the past.

➤ Lord, help me to maintain the right attitude when a prospect shows up.

➤ Father, give me the power to overcome temptations.

➤ Lord, forgive me for lack of self-control in my life.

➤ Father, I send the blood of Jesus into my foundation to cancel any covenants that are holding me back in singlehood, if it is not your plan for me.

➤ I command the fire of the Holy Ghost to purify my marital foundation.

➤ Lord, give the woman/man ordained by you to be my spouse no rest and no peace until they manifest.

➤ Let any token connecting me to my spiritual spouse burn by fire.

A call to repentance

To repent means to turn away from evil and to move toward a completely new direction. It is the key to forgiveness of sins. Without true repentance, men will all perish. You have the opportunity right now to repent of all evils you have ever done against the Lord, ignorantly or knowingly. If some of the truths revealed in this material have convicted you, then the Lord is asking you to repent. If your motive toward marriage has been wrong, then repent.

If you ignorantly placed a curse on yourself, then repent now. Without repentance, there is no true confession unto salvation. Repentance precedes confession, which now leads to forgiveness of sins. So I'm calling you to completely turn away and abandon evil lifestyles so that you will not only get married or enjoy the marriage, but also go to heaven.

Make up your mind today to become a true disciple of Christ because the days ahead of us are more evil than what you see right now. May the Lord Almighty bless you and enlarge your coast as you obey His voice. May He replenish and restore your marriage. I pray you will not get yourself into any wrong marriage and that you will remain a candidate for heaven in JESUS'S precious name. AMEN!

THE END

If you have more concerns and comments, you can contact us at jtway.international@gmail.com. You can also reach us for counseling on some of the issues mentioned in this material. Our goal is to bring men to salvation found in JESUS and to help them remain in true HOLINESS till the end.

SUBCRIBE TO our YouTube channel: Jesus the way international outreach.

Acknowledgements

I appreciate my wife for giving me the opportunity and freedom to write. Her support to this material as a wife and a mother was immensely vital.

Thank you, Dr. Eric Tangumonkem, for putting this book together.

I also appreciate all the editors and designers for doing a fantastic work on this material.

And many thanks to my precious divine Holy Spirit (my best teacher,helper,facilitator).

The author is available for speaking engagements:

If you want to invite Pastor Prosper Ehunyi to come and speak, you can call him using this number 7135769026/8324047837 or email him at pros4jesus@yahoo.com

IEM PRESS

To order additional copies of this book call:
214-908-3963
Or visit our website at
www.iempublishing.com

If you enjoyed this quality
custom-published book
Drop by our website for more
books and information

*"Inspiring, equipping and
motivating one author at a time."*